All about Rabbits

Written by Michèle Dufresne

PIONEER VALLEY EDUCATIONAL PRESS, INC.

Here is a **rabbit**.

It is a big rabbit.

Rabbits can be little or big. Some rabbits can be up to 4 feet long.

tail

ears
whiskers
leg

Here is a **baby** rabbit.
The baby rabbit is a kit.

A kit is born without fur,
and at first, it can't see.

Rabbits like to dig.
A rabbit can dig a **tunnel**.

Here is a rabbit.

Nip! Nip!

The rabbit bit the **grass.**

Rabbits eat only
plants. Rabbits like
grass, seeds, and roots.

Here is a rabbit.
The rabbit can sit.

A rabbit will sit very still so
that a predator does not see it.

glossary